# LANAI TRAVEL GUIDE

Itineraries, Outdoor Adventures, Beaches, Culinary Delights, and Hidden Gems- A Local's Guide to the Island's Top Sites and Tips

## Paul Bunyan

1| LANAI TRAVEL GUIDE

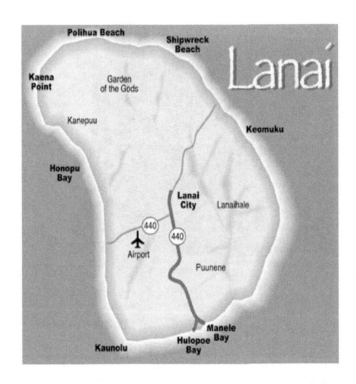

Polihua Beach

Shipwreck Beach

Lanaí

Kaena Point

Garden of the Gods

Kanepuu

Keomuku

Honopu Bay

Lanai City

Lanaihale

440

440

Airport

Puunene

Manele Bay

Kaunolu

Hulopoe Bay

# Contents

When billionaires are fighting over something, you know it's special. That's the case with Hawaii's most exclusive island, Lanai. Microsoft co-founder, Bill Gates, has been trying to lay his hands on some Lanai real estate for some time. Larry Ellison, founder of Oracle, took control of 97 percent of Lanai in 2012. But don't let this clash of titans stop you from visiting.

Here is where Mother Nature puts on quite a show, providing remote beaches, otherworldly rock formations and colorful underwater reefs. You'll probably need an off-roading vehicle and a taste for adventure to reach them – top sights like Shipwreck Beach and the Munro Trail are literally off the beaten (or paved) paths. Cool down from exploring the terrain at one of the area's posh hotels where you can expect to luxuriate in exceptional cuisine, first-class service and upscale accommodations. Should you crave more activity, you can try your hand at deep sea fishing, horseback riding, lawn bowling and more. With all this, how can you resist the coveted charms of tiny Lanai?

## Benefits of This Guide

Forget the limitations of conventional travel guides. This curated companion isn't merely a roadmap; it's a window into Lanai's soul, crafted to elevate your experience beyond the tourist veneer. Dive deeper, explore further, and discover an island that resonates, not just with sun-soaked vistas, but with a vibrant culture and hidden gems waiting to be unveiled. Here's why embarking on your Lanai journey with this dynamic resource will redefine your island escape:

1. **Curated Escapes, Not Tourist Traps:** Step off the beaten path and into secret havens. This book will guide you to untouched landscapes, vibrant coral reefs teeming with life, and secluded coves untouched by mass tourism. Imagine yourself immersed in the serene beauty of Pāʻao Bay, its volcanic formations whispering ancient stories, or savoring the authentic charm of Lanai City cafes where locals gather.

2. **Immerse in the Authentic Aloha:** Cultural understanding transcends mere descriptions. We connect you with the essence of Lanai, weaving its rich heritage into every recommendation. Envision yourself learning the graceful movements of hula from local dancers, witnessing the power of a traditional blessing ceremony,

or sharing laughter and stories with Lanai residents under the blanket of stars.

**3. Bespoke Adventures, Unforgettable Memories:** Unlike rigid itineraries, this guide empowers you to design an experience that speaks to your soul. Embark on challenging hikes, lose yourself on pristine beaches, or indulge in the luxury of private spa retreats. We provide the tools and insider knowledge to craft a Lanai adventure that is uniquely yours.

3. **Beyond the Picture-Perfect:** We invite you to go past stunning visuals and generic descriptions. Dive deep into evocative storytelling, painting a sensory picture of sights, sounds, and emotions that await. Imagine inhaling the invigorating ocean breeze as you discover a hidden waterfall, or the delectable sweetness of local pineapple as you explore the island's agricultural roots.

**4. Journey Responsibly, Connect Deeply:** We believe in fostering sustainable practices and respectful interactions with the island and its people. Leave no trace, support local businesses, and engage with the community in a meaningful way – your journey will be enriched, and Lanai will flourish.

Dive into its hidden stories, forge genuine connections, and create memories that transcend the ordinary. Remember, the most transformative journeys are often unplanned, fueled by curiosity and a desire to truly connect. Let this guide be your compass, not your script, and embark on an unforgettable Lanai adventure that whispers tales untold.

## Best Times to Visit Lanai

Lanai is best visited between June and November, when it is at its warmest and driest. However, the island's trade winds keep temperatures moderate all year, with highs in the mid-70s and lows in the mid-60s. Furthermore, because the island receives the least amount of precipitation (about 37 inches per year) of any Hawaiian island, rain rarely poses a danger. If you've come to Lanai for whale-watching season, schedule your vacation between January and April, which are the busiest months. The season formally begins in December and concludes in May. Remember that winter is the most popular time to visit Hawaii, so expect to pay a premium for travel and                                    accommodations.

## June-November

Lanai's summer and fall are distinguished by dry, mild weather. This time period coincides with hurricane season, albeit hurricanes are uncommon in Hawaii. From late summer until fall, you may be able to get a little reduction on hotel prices, but the savings will be minimal.

## Pineapple Festival (July) December - May

This is the best season to see whales off the coast of Lanai, but it is also the most expensive period to fly to Hawaii. Plan your whale-watching trip between January and April. Lanai's "winter" temps (low to mid-70s) are lower than the peak summer months (high 70s), but the weather is only slightly cooler and should not prevent you from visiting.

## Getting Around Lanai

The best way to move about Lanai is with a four-wheel drive car. This allows you to safely explore Lanai's 400 miles of unpaved roads, the majority of which are off-road trails. In comparison, the island has only 30 miles of paved road, which means that renting a car will not allow you to visit some of Lanai's most popular natural treasures. Taxis, albeit pricey, are also available. Inter-island travel is available via boat (to Maui)

or plane (to Oahu, Maui, Molokai, and the Big Island).

There are no direct flights from outside Hawaii to Lanai Airport (LNY), so you'll most likely need to connect through Honolulu or Maui. To get from the airport to your hotel, use a taxi. Before you arrive, check with your hotels to see whether they have shuttle service.

## Four-wheel-drive

Lanai's exotic scenery is best explored in a four-wheel-drive vchicle. Dollar Rent a Car and Lanai Cheap Jeep & Subaru Rentals both provide Jeep rentals in Lanai City. Prices vary based on the length of your rental, but you should reserve a vehicle in advance of your arrival to get the best deal. Some of Lanai's most popular sites, like as Shipwreck Bcach, Garden of the Gods, and the

Munro Trail, are easily accessible with your four-wheel-drive vehicle.

## Ferry

You can get to and from Maui by ferry. Ferries depart from Maui and Lanai five times daily, beginning in Lanai at 8 a.m. and ending at 5:45 p.m. One-way tickets are $30 for adults and $20 for youngsters. The ferry departs from Manele Harbor on Lanai and arrives at the loading pier in front of the Pioneer Inn on Maui. Trips over the Auau Channel take around an hour. If you're on the ferry between January and April, keep a look out for humpback whales.

## Plane

For speedy inter-island travel, take a plane. Hawaiian Airlines, along with other regional carriers such as Mokulele Airlines, fly to and from Lanai.

## What To Eat in Lanai

Lanai's charm extends beyond its captivating landscapes and vibrant culture. Nestled within its idyllic setting lies a diverse and delectable culinary scene, ready to tantalize your taste buds with locally sourced flavors, generations-old traditions, and modern interpretations. Join me on a gastronomic journey as i unveil the island's unique dining experiences, from hidden food trucks to oceanfront restaurants, each offering a distinct chapter in the story of Lunai's cuisine.

**Local Flavors: Authentic Indulgence**
- **Poke Bowls:** Experience the essence of Lunai through a poke bowl, featuring the island's bounty – fresh, locally caught ahi tuna marinated in savory sauces and presented on fluffy white rice adorned with crisp vegetables. Each bite bursts with freshness, echoing the island's fishing heritage and embodying the "poke" spirit of "to cut or slice."
- **Kalua Pork:** Immerse yourself in the rich aromas and textures of this traditional Hawaiian dish. Slow-cooked in an underground imu oven, the pork absorbs the earthy essence of volcanic soil, creating a unique and deeply satisfying culinary experience.
- **Laulau:** Unwrap the secrets of the sea with this island favorite. Layers of taro leaves embrace succulent fish or meat

seasoned with coconut milk and local herbs, creating a visually stunning and flavorful dish that reflects the island's culinary heritage.

**Restaurants: From Upscale Elegance to Island Charm**

- **Lanai City Grille:** Savor contemporary Hawaiian cuisine with breathtaking ocean vistas as your backdrop. Indulge in fresh seafood dishes, meticulously grilled meats, or vibrant vegetarian options, all crafted with locally sourced ingredients and presented with elegant finesse.
- **The Wharf:** Embark on a casual dining experience at this waterfront gem. Enjoy fresh seafood platters, pizzas crafted in a wood-fired oven, and refreshing tropical cocktails while the sun dips below the horizon, painting the sky in mesmerizing hues.
- **Cafe 560:** Immerse yourself in the local scene with this Lanai City staple. Sample hearty breakfast plates, mouthwatering

burgers, and refreshing smoothies, all served with a warm helping of aloha spirit and authentic island charm.

## Food Trucks: Culinary Gems on Wheels

- **Aloha Shrimp Truck:** Don't miss this island institution! Savor succulent garlic shrimp, savory fish tacos, and refreshing pineapple drinks, all served with genuine aloha spirit and a contagious sense of adventure.
- **Lanai Juice Truck:** Quench your thirst and nourish your body with freshly squeezed juices, smoothies made with locally sourced fruits, and healthy acai bowls, all crafted with a commitment to wellness and sustainability.
- **Lanai Tacos:** Embark on a culinary adventure with flavorful tacos filled with island-inspired ingredients like kalua pork, mahi-mahi, and fresh vegetables, all served with a side of homemade salsa and

guacamole, offering a delightful explosion of taste and texture.

## Markets: A Bounty of Freshness Awaits

- **Lanai Farmers Market:** Explore the vibrant heart of the island's agricultural community. Immerse yourself in stalls overflowing with colorful fruits and vegetables, locally sourced meats and seafood, and handcrafted souvenirs, all while engaging in warm conversations with friendly farmers and artisans.

- **Upcountry Farmers Market:** Experience the charm of upcountry living at this weekly market. Discover unique jams and jellies, locally made honey, and handcrafted gifts, all against the backdrop of breathtaking mountain vistas, creating a memorable and authentic experience.

Despite being Hawaii's smallest inhabited island, Lanai provides a varied selection of gastronomic delights. If you're on a tight budget and looking for a local hangout, check out Blue Ginger Café, which guests complimented for its burgers, homemade bread, and calm atmosphere. Pele's Other Garden Deli is also praised for its sandwiches and pizza. Coffee Works, one of the island's only coffee shops, is another must-stop if you need a cup of coffee and some souvenir coffee to take back to the mainland.

If you want to splurge, Lanai has you covered with a number of high-end resort establishments. Lanai City Bar & Grille at Hotel Lanai specializes on native cuisine, including venison, and has live music on the patio. Meanwhile, ONE FORTY, located at the picturesque Four Seasons Resort Lanai, serves wagyu beef and seasonal Hawaiian seafood. This is also where Lanai's own Nobu, the world-renowned sushi restaurant, can be found. Views, the lunch-only restaurant at the Manele Golf Course, completes Lanai's formal dining options with its (unsurprisingly) ocean views and Hawaiian tiny dishes (called pupus).

Visitors flock to Lanai seeking to experience secluded luxury. To heighten the sense of remoteness, go off-roading on your way to the island's best natural beauties. Polihua Beach and Shipwreck Beach on the northern shore have quiet sands that are ideal for romance. On the route, they might stop at the Garden of the Gods, a strange natural rock garden with numerous local stories. On the south side, visitors enjoy their time on the dunes of Hulopoe Bay and the fairways of the Manele Golf Course. To complete your perfect Hawaiian vacation, visit the Munro Trail, the only spot where you can see all six Hawaiian islands at once.

## 1. Hulopoe bay

Hulopoe Bay is one of Lanai's most popular beaches. Sunbathers enjoy the long stretches of sand, while snorkelers enjoy the colorful reefs teeming with fish and local plant life. This is one of the few beaches on Lanai that allows swimming, but only in the summer; the waves are too dangerous in the winter. If you're visiting

Lanai during the winter, a visit to Hulopoe Bay is still worthwhile because you can occasionally see dolphins and humpback whales from the shore.

Find sea stars and hermit crabs in the bay's eastern tide pools and picnicking in the shady regions behind the beach. If you get tired of sunbathing, put on your hiking shoes and take a 15- to 20-minute stroll along the cliffs immediately southeast of the tide pools to see Puu Pehe, also known as Sweetheart Rock. According to Hawaiian tradition, a bereaved warrior plunged from this 80-foot rock upon learning of his wife's death.

The beach, which is free to use, provides public BBQ grills, showers, and restrooms. Hulopoe Bay is located on Lanai's south shore, near the Four Seasons Resort Lanai.

## 2. Munro Trail

The Munro Trail is a convoluted 12.8-mile path that provides the sole opportunity to see all six Hawaiian islands at once - on a particularly clear day. Travelers can marvel at the ever-changing vistas of the forest, canyon, and ocean. When you reach the summit, you will see Lanai's tallest point, Lanaihale (House of Lanai), which stands at 3,370 feet.

Many Lanai tourists say that traversing the trail was the highlight of their vacation. It's also worth noting that, while hiking and biking are options, the majority of people utilize a Jeep.

Before beginning on your tour, consult a knowledgeable local or your hotel concierge. Munro Trail, located in the island's middle, can become impassable during heavy rains. The trail begins approximately north of Lanai City and ends at the Palawai Basin. The entire trip will take you two to three hours by automobile, depending on road conditions and how frequently you stop for photos. Remember that there are no amenities along the trail, so bring lots of water, food, and a full tank of gas. There is no charge to access the route.

### 3. Garden of Gods

When you think of "Garden of the Gods," you expect lush foliage, but not here. This arid region, also known as Keahiakawelo, is home to only irregularly formed stones and dust. So, why should you go to this seeming wasteland? First, the terrain appears to be as close to Mars as you will ever get. Second, at sunset, the orange light transforms the rocks into flaming reds and vivid purples. According to Hawaiian tradition, the dry terrain sprang from a challenge between two priests who were entrusted with keeping a fire going on their respective islands for longer than the other. The winner would be rewarded with a bounty of plants. To keep up with his rival, the Lanai priest burned all of the available foliage to keep his fires going, resulting in the arid country that exists today.

The drive to Garden of the Gods as exciting yet worthwhile. I suggest going after stopping at Polihua Beach because the two locations are so near. Travelers called the vistas "surreal" and "amazing." On a clear day, you can see the islands of Molokai and Oahu.

The Garden of the Gods is located about 6 miles northwest of Lanai City on the Polihua Trail.

Even if you use a four-wheel-drive car to handle the muddy road, it will take roughly 45 minutes to reach the spot. It is completely free to visit.

## 4. Dolphin and Whale Watching Tours

Humpback whales can be seen on all Hawaiian islands (the warm, shallow seas attract them), but the Auau Channel between Maui, Molokai, and Lanai is one of the world's top whale-watching spots. If you come between December and May, you may be able to see these gorgeous creatures from the shore, but for the greatest views, book a trip.

Your hotel may provide whale-watching excursions, but there are other tour companies that depart from Maui. This will require you to take the ferry to Maui, but previous visitors say it's an experience you shouldn't miss. Ultimate Whale Watch & Snorkel, Hawaii Ocean Rafting, and Sail Trilogy all receive good marks from visitors. Tours departing from Maui's Lahaina Harbor normally run around two hours. Prices vary by firm, but plan to spend at least $50 per adult. Some tour boats also include a hydrophone, which allows guests to hear whales underwater.

Keep in mind that whale-watching tours are only available from December through May. To learn more about price and booking, go to each company's website.

## 5. Manele Golf Course

The Manele Golf Course, created by the famed Jack Nicklaus, is located along Lanai's southern coast and amazes golfers with its difficulty and architecture. The course features lush greenery, ocean cliffs, beachfront fairways, and the occasional whale sighting (particularly during the winter, when whales pass through the bay).

Previous visitors enthused about the Manele Golf Course's great service and "breathtaking" views, and they recommended that travelers eat at the Views restaurant after their game.

Guests staying at the Four Seasons Resort Lanai, one of the island's premier beach resorts, receive preferential pricing, with 18-hole, nine-hole, and junior rates available. PGA professionals and a retail outlet offer a wide range of programs and lessons. A tee time costs approximately $350 per person.

## 6. Polihua Beach

Polihua Beach, about a 30-minute drive from the Garden of the Gods on the island's northern shore, is popular with visitors looking for a romantic environment for sunbathing or beachcombing. Sea turtles used to nest on this secluded two-mile stretch of sand. These endangered species are now extremely rare to see. In fact, many recent visitors report being the only ones here, whether human or animal. However, if you visit between December and April, you're likely to see migratory humpback whales from the coast.

Swimming is not recommended here due to high gusts and currents, and there are no restrooms. Access is free at all times, but going after sunset is discouraged.

## 7. Shipwreck Beach

Getting to Shipwreck Beach (also known as Kaiolohia) isn't easy. However, visitors who visit this unique location on the island's northeastern shore are treated to a memorable photo opportunity. There are two World War II ships that were purposefully grounded here. Most people come to see the YOGN-42, a fuel barge visible off the coast of Kaiolohia Bay. Another wreck, the YO-21 oiler, can be found 6 miles to the west of Awalua Bay.

This beach is not suitable for swimming or sunbathing, I highly recommend making the trip for the hike and views alone. However, they warn that you will encounter mountains of rubbish and debris that have washed ashore. If you wish to help the ecosystem, consider bringing a garbage bag to help with the cleanup. Also, if you are not in a four-wheel-drive vehicle, do not attempt to drive on the sand; you will become stuck and will have to be towed.

Shipwreck Beach is less than ten kilometers north of Lanai City. Take the Keomoku Highway past the Lodge at Koele. From there, turn right onto Keomoku Road (Highway 430). To get to the beach, you'll drive down a dirt road and then hike a short distance. Before leaving, check with your concierge for exact directions. Because the route involves driving on unpaved roads, four-wheel-drive vehicles are strongly recommended. Access is free 24 hours a day, seven days a week, though visiting at night is not recommended.

## 8. Lanai Cultural & Heritage Center

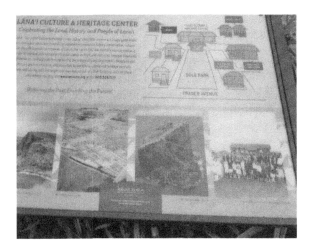

The nonprofit Lāna'i Culture & Heritage Center was established in 2007 to conserve and promote the island's culture and heritage. There is no other entity wholly committed to this mission. Educational activities and events are available throughout the year. The museum is open for special occasions. As a 501c3 charity, all initiatives to sustain Lāna'i's history, including the safeguarding of its historical collections with thousands of items, are sponsored by friends like you.

## 9. The Lanai Cat Sanctuary

Do you miss your cat from home? Don't miss Lanai's outdoor sanctuary, a joyful place for spayed and neutered cats. Imagine a big playground in paradise where over 600 cats frolic in the sun and nap under shady trees. Purring cats of all sizes and shapes eagerly anticipate your arrival. The caregivers, who enjoy caring for the cats, would also want to meet you. They enjoy matching people that want to adopt cats!

## 10.     The Mike Carroll Gallery

Mike Carroll Gallery is set among the towering Cook Pines of Dole Park in old Lana'i City. Mike and his other award-winning guest artists' unique paintings are on display, as well as fine art photography, handcrafted jewelry, bowls made from local woods, and an unexpected selection of Asian antiques. Discover why they've been dubbed "one of Hawaii's most beautiful galleries!" Open seven days a week (Mon-Sun 10am-6pm)

## 11. Sweetheart Rock

This unusual rock structure is a short walk from Manele Bay and the Four Seasons Hotel. The view of the rock and the surrounding cliff is breathtaking. The surrounding ocean environment and tidal pools teeming with marine life also evoke memories of past Hawaii visits. The rock's mythology, which features star-crossed lovers, contributes to the area's appeal and mystique. There is an old Hawaiian stone memorial on the rock that appears to date back to ancient times.

## 12.  The Manele Small Boat Harbor

The passenger ferry from Lahaina arrives here. The harbor facilities are excellent, featuring a huge restroom, a nice store, and a covered shelter. The gorgeous Manele beach is just a short walk from the harbor (12-15 minutes). The short, lovely route to Sweetheart Rock leads from the beach.

## 1. Four Seasons Resort Lanai

**Address: 1 Manele Bay Rd, Lanai City, Lanai, HI 96763**

## Top Amenities

- Free Wi-Fi
- Free Parking
- Business Center
- Restaurants
- Pets Allowed
- Pools

This Four Seasons facility is popular among beachgoers. This resort, located on a lovely length of Hulopoe Bay sand facing the Pacific Ocean, provides breathtaking ocean views, well-kept gardens, and excellent customer service. Guests can spend their time outdoors doing things like snorkeling, deep-sea fishing, hiking, whale viewing, scuba diving, and more. The property is described by visitors as "paradise" and "heaven on earth". All guest rooms have private patios and have amenities such as 75-inch flat-screen TVs with Blu-ray players, Nespresso machines, and complimentary internet access. One of the most popular amenities is the complimentary shuttle that transports you to and from Lanai Town. Recent visitors warn that meals at the resort's several restaurants and spa treatments will be expensive. Still, most visitors like the Four Seasons resort's beachfront location and world-class golf course.

## 2. Sensei Lanai, a Four Seasons resort

**Address:**1 Keomoku Highway, Lanai City, Lanai, HI 96763

## Top Amenities

- Free Wi-Fi
- Free Parking
- Business Center
- Restaurants
- Pools

This Four Seasons resort, located in the heart of Lanai, Hawaii's smallest populated island, exudes elegance. Travelers arrive at the resort on a semi-private jet from Honolulu, with a range of activities to make each stay memorable and distinctive. Previous guests have raved about Sensei Lanai's central location, pleasant staff, and relaxing setting. Visitors will like the neutral design and natural light in their guest rooms, which also have marble accents, in-room iPads, and trademark bath treatments. The hotel is an adults-only establishment, so guests can expect a quiet stay, and the on-site spa, salon, outdoor hot tubs, and pool will help them relax. The resort also provides a variety of active activities for guests, such as scuba diving excursions, horseback riding tours, cooking workshops, and cultural education programs. Although Sensei Lanai does not have a golf course, tennis facilities, or beach access, the hotel does provide a free shuttle to its sister resort, Four Seasons Resort Lanai, which is less than 10 miles south and has those attractions. When returning to Sensei Lanai, guests can dine either the hotel's

Japanese fusion restaurant, Sensei by Nobu, or the more casual Koele Garden Bar.

### 3. Hotel Lanai

**Address:828 Lanai Avenue, Lanai City, Lanai, HI 96763**

## Top Amenities

- Free parking
- Free High-Speed Internet (WiFi)
- Free breakfast
- Car hire
- Baggage storage
- Outdoor furniture

The Hotel Lanai is an island landmark located in the heart of Lanai City. The hotel was recently remodeled in 2018 and now offers modern, attractive accommodations and services for tourists looking for a quiet hideaway on Lanai. The 11-room property, just steps from Dole Park, welcomes visitors from all over the world to experience gorgeous garden views, genuine Hawaiian hospitality, and island food at the on-site neighborhood restaurant, Lanai City Bar & Grille.

## 4. Montage Kapalua Bay

**Address:** 1 Bay Drive, Kapalua, Maui, HI 96761-9035

## Top Amenities:

- Oceanfront location
- Multiple pools
- Spa
- Fitness center,
- Multiple dining options
- Kids' club
- Golf course access

Located on neighboring Maui, this luxurious resort offers breathtaking ocean views, spacious accommodations, and top-notch amenities. Take a dip in the infinity pool, pamper yourself at the spa, or tee off on the world-renowned Kapalua Bay Golf Course. With its family-friendly facilities and endless activities, this resort is ideal for a multi-island adventure.

## 5. Four Seasons Resort Maui at Wailea, Lanai Hawaii

**Address: 3900 Wailea Alanui Dr, Wailea, HI 96753**

## Top Amenities

- Multiple pools
- Multiple dining options
- Spa,
- Fitness center,
- kids' club
- Cultural activities
- Access to Wailea Beach

Experience the epitome of luxury at this award-winning resort situated on Maui's beautiful Wailea Beach. Relax by the oceanfront pool, savor gourmet cuisine, or explore the vibrant coral reefs just offshore. With its extensive amenities and activities, this resort caters to every vacation wish.

## 6. Lanai Oceanfront Condos, Lanai Hawaii

**Address: 925 Fleming Ave, Lanai City, HI 96773**

### Top Amenities:

- Budget-friendly rates
- Ocean views
- Private balconies
- Full kitchens in all units
- Outdoor pool
- Laundry facilities

Enjoy comfortable accommodations and stunning ocean views without breaking the bank at this condo complex. Prepare meals in your full kitchen, relax on your private balcony, and take a refreshing dip in the pool. This property is a great option for budget-conscious travelers who want to be close to the beach.

## 7. Kaunoa Resort, Lanai Hawaii

**Address: 565 Lanai Ave, Lanai City, HI 96773**

### Top Amenities:

- Affordable rates
- Central location
- Outdoor pool
- Laundry facilities
- BBQ area

This mid-range hotel offers comfortable accommodations in a convenient location within walking distance of shops and restaurants. Relax by the pool, prepare meals in the shared kitchen, and explore the island at your own pace. This hotel is a good choice for value-seeking travelers who want to be in the heart of the action.

## Lanai's Nightlife

Sunsets unveil a different side of Lunai, as the island trades its daytime charm for a more relaxed, intimate energy. While not a bustling party scene, Lanai offers a unique tapestry of nightlife experiences, each infused with the island's signature aloha spirit and distinct local flavor. Let us shed light on the hidden gems and vibrant offerings that await you under the starry Lanai sky.

**Sunset Serenades & Oceanfront Cocktails:**

- **One Forty:** Savor handcrafted cocktails and tapas-style plates as the sun dips below the horizon, painting the sky in fiery hues. Live music fills the air with gentle melodies, setting the mood for a romantic evening and unforgettable conversations.
- **Lanai City Grille:** Enjoy breathtaking ocean views while sipping on tropical cocktails or local beers. Catch the occasional live music performance featuring talented local musicians, creating a captivating blend of island vibes and sophisticated ambiance.
- **The Wharf:** As the moon replaces the sun, this oceanfront gem transforms into a lively gathering spot. Share laughter and stories over refreshing drinks and light bites, all while enjoying the gentle ocean breeze and the mesmerizing night sky.

**Local Haunts & Cultural Immersions:**

- **Lanai City Bar & Grill:** Mingle with the locals at this friendly neighborhood bar. Enjoy classic pub fare, sip on local beers, and engage in lively conversations about island life, gaining unique insights into Lunai's heart and soul.
- **Pele's Other Place:** Experience the spirit of "Talk Story" at this local watering hole. Share stories with fellow travelers and friendly locals, learn about the island's past and present, and soak in the authentic island atmosphere.
- **Stargazing at Keomuku:** Escape the light pollution and ascend to the island's highest point. Observe the Milky Way unfold in all its celestial glory, and listen to local storytellers share ancient legends and myths under the starlit sky, creating a truly magical experience.

**Live Music & Cultural Performances:**

- **Lanai Cultural Center:** Experience the vibrant tapestry of Polynesian culture through traditional hula performances and mesmerizing storytelling sessions. Immerse yourself in the rhythmic melodies and graceful movements, gaining a deeper appreciation for the island's rich heritage.
- **Lanai Pineapple Company Events:** Throughout the year, the company hosts special events featuring live music, local artisans, and delicious food offerings. Immerse yourself in the island's agricultural heritage while enjoying lively entertainment and a genuine sense of community.
- **Full Moon Drum Circle:** Gather on the beach under the glow of the full moon and join a rhythmic celebration. Feel the beat of the drums resonate within you, connect with the natural world, and create a shared experience that transcends words.

Lunai isn't just a visual feast; it's a sanctuary for your soul, a haven where tranquility washes over you like the tide lapping the shore. Whether you seek pampering rejuvenation or an active embrace of nature, the island offers a diverse tapestry of wellness experiences designed to revitalize your mind, body, and spirit.

## Spas: Where Indulgence Meets Tranquility

- **Sense, a Rosewood Spa:** Surrender to ultimate pampering within this luxurious haven. Immerse yourself in a signature massage using locally sourced botanicals, unwind in a hydrotherapy pool overlooking the ocean, or indulge in a bespoke facial leaving your skin radiant.
- **Four Seasons Resort Lanai Spa:** Nestled amidst serene gardens, this sanctuary offers rejuvenating treatments inspired by ancient Hawaiian healing practices. Unwind with a lomi lomi massage using warm volcanic stones, or

soothe your soul with a coconut milk and kukui nut body wrap, rediscovering inner peace.

- **Pūʻu Pehe Yoga & Massage:** Connect with nature and yourself at this unique retreat perched on a volcanic cone. Enjoy a rejuvenating massage infused with essential oils sourced from the island's flora, followed by a restorative yoga session overlooking breathtaking vistas.

## Yoga Retreats: Reconnecting with Your Inner Self

- **Sunrise Yoga at Hulopoe Beach:** Greet the day with a rejuvenating yoga practice on the pristine sands of Hulopoe Beach. Feel the cool ocean breeze kiss your skin, absorb the golden glow of the rising sun, and let the rhythmic waves guide your movements into deep relaxation.
- **Mindfulness Retreat at Lanai Cat Sanctuary:** Immerse yourself in a transformative experience combining

yoga, meditation, and the soothing presence of rescued cats. Connect with your inner self, cultivate compassion, and discover the healing power of human-animal connection.

- **Full Moon Meditation at Pāʻao Bay:** Escape the light pollution and find solace under the glow of the full moon at this secluded bay. Guided meditation amidst the tranquil ocean whispers and gentle sea breeze will leave you feeling centered and deeply connected to nature.

## Outdoor Activities: Nature's Embrace

- **Stand-up Paddleboarding at Kaʻena Point:** Glide across the serene waters, surrounded by dramatic lava rock formations and vibrant marine life. Witness playful dolphins dancing alongside you, and breathe in the invigorating ocean air, leaving you feeling energized and rejuvenated.
- **Hiking to Waiʻalae Iki Hike:** Immerse yourself in the lush rainforest on this

moderate hike. Discover hidden waterfalls, cascading streams, and vibrant flora, each step immersing you deeper into the island's serene embrace.

- **Horseback Riding at Lanai Ranch:** Connect with the land and its spirit on a horseback riding adventure through rolling hills and scenic trails. Breathe in the fresh air, feel the rhythmic hoofbeats beneath you, and let the island's beauty wash over your soul.

Embarking on a Lunai adventure should be filled with carefree joy and unforgettable experiences. To ensure a smooth and healthy journey, let's address some essential aspects of health and safety:

## Travel Insurance: Securing Peace of Mind

While accidents and unforeseen circumstances are rarely anticipated, having travel insurance offers valuable peace of mind. Consider coverage that includes medical expenses, trip cancellation, lost luggage, and emergency evacuation. Research plans, compare benefits, and choose one that aligns with your budget and activities.

## Healthcare Information: Knowing Where to Turn

Lanai Community Health Center provides primary care services for both residents and visitors. For emergencies, Lanai City First

Responders handle ambulance services and transport to Maui Memorial Medical Center, a well-equipped facility with a range of specialists. Familiarize yourself with these resources and their locations before your trip.

## Sun Protection: Embracing the Sunshine Responsibly

Lunai's sunshine beckons, but remember, moderation is key. Pack broad-spectrum sunscreen with SPF 30 or higher and reapply frequently, especially after swimming or sweating. Seek shade during peak sun hours (10 am to 4 pm) and consider protective clothing, hats, and sunglasses. Minimize dehydration by carrying reusable water bottles and staying hydrated throughout the day.

## Photography Tips

Lunai's breathtaking landscapes, vibrant culture, and warm-hearted people are begging to be captured through your lens. Here are some tips to ensure your photos radiate the island's unique charm:

- **Embrace the Golden Hour:** Schedule your outdoor photography sessions during sunrise or sunset, also known as the "golden hour." The soft, warm light bathes the landscapes in a magical glow, adding depth and dimension to your shots.

- **Seek Contrasts and Textures:** Look for contrasting elements in your composition, like the turquoise ocean against rugged lava rocks or lush green rainforests against vibrant bougainvillea blossoms. Textures like weathered wood, volcanic rock formations, and flowing waterfalls add visual interest.
- **Capture the Essence of Aloha:** Don't just photograph landscapes; capture the spirit of the island and its people. Engage with locals, capture their genuine smiles and welcoming expressions, and document cultural activities like hula dancing or lei making.
- **Embrace Different Perspectives:** Experiment with different angles and vantage points. Get low to capture the vastness of the ocean, climb a hill for

panoramic vistas, or lie down to photograph wildflowers from a unique perspective.

- **Utilize Natural Light:** Whenever possible, rely on natural light for a more authentic and vibrant feel. Diffused sunlight through clouds or filtered through leaves can create stunning effects.
- **People Photography Etiquette:** Always ask permission before photographing people, especially when capturing close-up portraits. A genuine smile and respectful approach can go a long way.
- **Essential Gear:** Pack a lens hood to protect your lens from dust and stray water droplets. A polarizing filter can reduce glare and enhance colors. A tripod is helpful for low-light photography and long exposures.
- **Beyond the Technical:** Remember, the most captivating photos often capture emotions and stories. Look for moments that evoke joy, serenity, or cultural

significance. Let your photos tell a story about your Lunai experience, not just showcase its beauty.

**Bonus Tips:**
- Carry a portable charger to ensure your camera stays powered throughout the day.
- Pack a lens cleaning cloth and a small dust blower to keep your lens clear.
- Research local photography regulations and restrictions, especially regarding drone usage.
- Most importantly, have fun and experiment! Don't be afraid to break the rules and capture Lunai's magic through your unique lens.

### Essential Phrases for Your Lunai Adventure: Aloha & Beyond!

While English is widely spoken on Lunai, learning a few basic Hawaiian phrases will add a touch of aloha to your interactions and deepen your connection to the island's culture. Here are some essential words and phrases to get you started:

**Greetings:**
- **Aloha:** Hello, goodbye, love, peace (most versatile word)
- **Aloha kakahiaka:** Good morning
- **Aloha awakea:** Good late morning
- **Aloha auinala:** Good afternoon
- **Aloha ahiahi:** Good evening
- **Mahalo:** Thank you
- **Mahalo nui loa:** Thank you very much
- **A hui hou:** Until we meet again

**Basic Communication:**
- **'Ae:** Yes
- **'A'ole:** No
- **Pehea 'oe?** How are you?

- **Maika'i nō wau:** I'm good. (Formal)
- **A'ole maika'i:** I'm not good. (Formal)
- **Pehea 'oe kāua?** How are you? (Informal)
- 'A'ole pilikia: You're welcome. (Informal)
- **Kū mai:** Come here.
- **Noho iho:** Sit down.
- **He mea 'ono:** It's delicious.
- **Komo mai:** Welcome in.
- **E kala mai:** Please.

## Directions & Locations:
- **Mauka:** Towards the mountains
- **Makai:** Towards the ocean
- **Hehi:** Right
- **Mahele:** Left
- **Ma waho:** Outside
- **Ma loko:** Inside
- **Wai:** Water
- **Holoholo:** Go
- **Ka'u:** My
- *'Ou:** Your

**Cultural Phrases:**
- **Malama pono:** Take care, respect the land and people.
- **Mau loa:** Forever, always.
- **Hoʻihoʻi:** Return, come back again.
- **ʻAʻohe mea kaumaha:** No worries.
- **Mahalo nui loa no ka ʻoluolu:** Thank you very much for your kindness.

**Bonus Tip:** Learn the pronunciation of the ʻokina (ʻ) and the kahakō (ā, ē, ī, ō, ū). They can significantly change the meaning of a word.

## A Customized 48-Hour Itinerary

Lanai, an island adorned with pristine beaches, volcanic wonders, and rich cultural heritage, awaits your exploration. While this two-day itinerary provides a foundation, remember, the most captivating chapters of your Lanai story are yet to be written. Consider this a personalized canvas, ready to be filled with experiences that resonate with your unique desires.

**Day 1: Immerse in Natural Grandeur and Local Spirit**

- **Morning:** Begin your journey at **Hulopoe Bay**. Bathe in its turquoise embrace, snorkel vibrant coral reefs teeming with life, or simply relax on the pristine sand. For an unforgettable encounter, consider a guided swim alongside gentle manta rays (season permitting).
- **Lunch:** Immerse yourself in the local spirit at a Lanai City café. **Pele's Other Place** offers authentic island flavors, while **Blue Ginger Café** infuses local ingredients with creative flair.
- **Afternoon:** Embark on the **Munro Trail**. This moderate hike rewards with panoramic vistas, ancient petroglyphs whispering tales of the past, and lush rainforest landscapes.

- **Sunset:** Witness the **Garden of Gods** transform as the setting sun paints its volcanic rock formations in a fiery spectacle. This surreal landscape guarantees memorable photographs.
- **Dinner:** Savor fresh seafood and breathtaking oceanfront views at **The Wharf**. Let the exquisite cuisine and panoramic setting enhance your evening.
- **Evening:** Delve into Hawaiian culture at the **Lanai Cultural & Heritage Center**. Immerse yourself in storytelling, music, and captivating hula performances that resonate with the island's vibrant heritage.

## Day 2: Embrace Adventures and Serene Moments

- **Morning:** Challenge yourself on the **Manele Golf Course**, designed by the legendary Jack Nicklaus. Whether you're an avid golfer or simply seeking scenic walks, the manicured grounds and ocean vistas offer a unique experience (reservations recommended).

- **Lunch:** Pack a picnic and head to the secluded **Polihua Beach**. Discover its vastness, observe playful spinner dolphins in their natural habitat, and enjoy a tranquil swim in the turquoise waters.
- **Afternoon:** Explore the dramatic volcanic coastline at **Shipwreck Beach**. Search for remnants of a historic shipwreck, marvel at the rugged beauty, and uncover hidden coves untouched by mass tourism.
- **Sunset:** Allow yourself to unwind at your accommodation's pool or beach, reflecting on your day's adventures and the island's captivating beauty.
- **Evening:** Visit the **Lanai Cat Sanctuary**. Volunteer with these furry friends, learn about responsible pet ownership, and let their playful energy rejuvenate your spirit.

**Personalize Your Narrative:**

- **Beach Enthusiast:** Instead of hiking, spend more time exploring Hulopoe, Shipwreck, or discover hidden gems like Ka'āpu Cove.
- **Cultural Aficionado:** Participate in a lei-making workshop, immerse yourself in the vibrant energy of a luau, or embark on a stargazing expedition to Keomuku Peak.
- **Adventure Seeker:** Embark on a guided kayak tour along the coastline, test your balance on a stand-up paddleboard, or rent mountain bikes for an off-road exploration.
- **Family Fun:** Plan a picnic at Pā'ao Bay, embark on a scavenger hunt for petroglyphs on the Munro Trail, or visit the Pineapple Company for interactive exhibits that entertain young minds.

# 4-Day Itinerary

Aloha! Prepare to be captivated by the vibrant tapestry of Lanai, an island where pristine beaches, volcanic wonders, and rich cultural heritage intertwine. This curated itinerary provides a framework for your 4-day adventure, crafted to ignite your curiosity and personalize your exploration. Remember, the most captivating chapters of your Lanai story are yet to be written. Consider this a canvas, ready to be filled with experiences that resonate with your unique desires.

## Day 1: Unveiling Natural Beauty & Immerse in Culture

- **Morning:** Begin your Lanai experience at the iconic **Hulopoe Bay**. Bask in the turquoise embrace of its pristine waters, explore vibrant coral reefs teeming with life, or join a guided swim alongside gentle manta rays (season permitting).
- **Lunch:** Immerse yourself in the local spirit at a Lanai City café. **Pele's Other Place** offers authentic island flavors,

while **Blue Ginger Café** infuses local ingredients with creative flair.

- **Afternoon:** Challenge yourself on the moderate **Munro Trail**, rewarded with panoramic vistas, ancient petroglyphs whispering tales of the past, and lush rainforest landscapes.
- **Sunset:** Witness the **Garden of Gods** transform as the setting sun paints its volcanic rock formations in a fiery spectacle. Capture breathtaking photographs while soaking in the awe-inspiring scenery.
- **Evening:** Delve into Hawaiian heritage at the **Lanai Cultural & Heritage Center**. Immerse yourself in storytelling, music, and captivating hula performances that resonate with the island's vibrant culture.

## Day 2: Adventure & Artistic Encounters
- **Morning:** Embrace your artistic side at **The Mike Carroll Gallery**, where a diverse collection of local and

international artwork awaits your exploration.

- **Lunch:** Pack a picnic for a serene afternoon at **Polihua Beach**. Discover its vastness, observe playful spinner dolphins in their natural habitat, and enjoy a refreshing swim in the turquoise waters.
- **Afternoon:** Embark on a guided kayak tour along the dramatic coastline, offering unique perspectives and potential snorkeling opportunities among vibrant coral reefs.
- **Sunset:** Witness the iconic silhouette of **Sweetheart Rock** bathed in the warm glow of the setting sun. Learn the local legend associated with this natural wonder and capture unforgettable photographs.
- **Evening:** Enjoy live music and delectable fare at **The Wharf**, followed by a captivating stargazing experience on the beach. Alternatively, visit the **Lanai Cat Sanctuary** for heartwarming

interactions with furry friends and learn about responsible pet ownership.

**Day 3: Luxurious Golf & Hidden Secrets**
- **Morning:** Tee off on the world-renowned **Manele Golf Course** designed by the legendary Jack Nicklaus (reservations recommended). Even non-golfers can appreciate the scenic walks and breathtaking ocean vistas.
- **Lunch:** Indulge in gourmet cuisine and panoramic ocean views at the elegant **One Forty** restaurant.
- **Afternoon:** Choose your relaxation destination: unwind at your resort's pool or beach, or embark on a journey to discover hidden coves like Pā'ao Bay, known for its tranquility and cultural significance.
- **Sunset:** Immerse yourself in the vibrant energy of a traditional luau at a beachfront resort. Savor delicious island cuisine, witness captivating hula dances, and

experience the warmth of Polynesian culture under the starry sky.

## Day 4: Memories & Farewell

- **Morning:** Visit the bustling **Manele Small Boat Harbor** and witness the return of fishing boats with their fresh catch. Enjoy breakfast at a harborfront cafe, soaking in the vibrant atmosphere.
- **Lunch:** Pack a final picnic for an adventure at **Shipwreck Beach**. Explore its unique volcanic landscape, search for remnants of the historical shipwreck, and soak in the sun before your departure.
- **Afternoon:** Immerse yourself in the charming Lanai City, browsing local shops for unique souvenirs that capture the essence of your island adventure.
- **Farewell:** As you depart Lanai, reflect on the experiences that touched you, the memories you created, and the spirit of Aloha that continues to resonate within you.

## Personalize Your Exploration:

- **Beach Lover:** Dedicate more time to swimming, snorkeling, or kayaking at various beaches.
- **Cultural Buff:** Attend a lei-making workshop, participate in a cultural tour, or visit historical sites like Keomuku Peak for a deeper understanding of Hawaiian heritage.
- **Adventure Seeker:** Hike Kahekili's Peak, go off-roading in a Jeep, or try stand-up paddleboarding for an adrenaline rush.
- **Family Fun:** Build sandcastles, explore tide pools, visit the Pineapple Company for interactive exhibits, or enjoy family-friendly activities at resorts.

# 7-Day Immersion

Aloha! Embrace the captivating tapestry of Lanai, where pristine beaches, volcanic wonders, and rich cultural heritage intertwine. This meticulously crafted 7-day itinerary ignites your curiosity and empowers you to personalize your island adventure. Remember, the most captivating chapters of your Lanai story are yet to be written. Consider this a canvas, ready to be filled with experiences that resonate with your unique desires.

## Day 1: Unveiling Natural Beauty & Immerse in Culture

- Begin your Lanai experience at the iconic Hulopoe Bay. Bask in its turquoise embrace, explore vibrant coral reefs teeming with life, or embark on a guided swim alongside gentle manta rays (season permitting). Invigorate your palate with a delectable lunch at a Lanai City café, immersing yourself in the local spirit.
- Challenge yourself on the moderate Munro Trail, rewarded with panoramic

vistas, ancient petroglyphs whispering tales of the past, and lush rainforest landscapes.
- Witness the magical transformation of the Garden of Gods as the setting sun paints its volcanic rock formations in a fiery spectacle. Capture awe-inspiring photographs while soaking in the breathtaking scenery.
- Delve into the vibrant Hawaiian heritage at the Lanai Cultural & Heritage Center. Immerse yourself in storytelling, music, and captivating hula performances that resonate with the island's soul.

## Day 2: Adventures & Artistic Encounters
- Explore the quaint shops and charming atmosphere of Lanai City. Savor breakfast at a local joint and browse unique island-inspired souvenirs, capturing the essence of Lanai's cultural tapestry.
- Embark on a guided kayak tour along the dramatic coastline, offering unique perspectives and potential snorkeling

opportunities among vibrant coral reefs. Immerse yourself in the island's artistic spirit with a visit to The Mike Carroll Gallery, exploring its diverse collection of local and international artwork.

- Witness the iconic silhouette of Sweetheart Rock bathed in the warm glow of the setting sun. Learn the local legend associated with this natural wonder and capture unforgettable photographs before enjoying live music and delectable fare at The Wharf. Conclude the evening with a captivating stargazing experience under the clear skies.

## Day 3: Luxurious Golf & Hidden Secrets

- Tee off on the world-renowned Manele Golf Course, designed by the legendary Jack Nicklaus. Even non-golfers can appreciate the scenic walks and breathtaking ocean vistas. Indulge in gourmet cuisine and panoramic ocean views at the elegant One Forty restaurant for a truly memorable lunch experience.

- Discover the serenity of hidden coves like Pāʻao Bay, known for its tranquility and cultural significance. Kayak, swim, or simply relax on the beach, embracing the tranquility of this secluded haven.

**Day 4: Unwind & Explore**
- Rejuvenate your mind and body at your resort's spa, treating yourself to a pampering massage or traditional Hawaiian therapy.
- Immerse yourself in the bustling atmosphere of the Manele Small Boat Harbor, witnessing the return of fishing boats with their fresh catch. Enjoy breakfast at a harborfront cafe, soaking in the vibrant atmosphere.
- Visit the Lanai Cat Sanctuary, interacting with furry friends and learning about responsible pet ownership. Engage with the community and immerse yourself in the spirit of Aloha.
- Celebrate the evening with a traditional luau at a beachfront resort. Savor

delicious island cuisine, witness captivating hula dances, and experience the warmth of Polynesian culture under the starry sky.

## Day 5: Exploring the Rugged Coast & Local Flavors

- Embark on an unforgettable Jeep tour along the rugged north shore, experiencing breathtaking landscapes and secluded beaches like Kaʻāpu Cove and Shark Bay. Discover hidden gems and immerse yourself in the island's raw beauty.
- Pack a picnic for a secluded and adventurous afternoon at Shipwreck Beach. Explore its unique volcanic landscape, search for remnants of the historical shipwreck, and enjoy a refreshing swim in the turquoise waters.

## Days 6 & 7: Tailor Your Exploration

With two remaining days, craft your unique adventure based on your preferences:

- **Beach Lover:** Dedicate more time to swimming, snorkeling, or kayaking at various beaches.
- **Cultural Buff:** Attend a lei-making workshop, participate in a cultural tour, or visit historical sites like Keomuku Peak for a deeper understanding of Hawaiian heritage.
- **Adventure Seeker:** Hike Kahekili's Peak, go off-roading in a Jeep, or try stand-up paddleboarding for an adrenaline rush.
- **Family Fun:** Build sandcastles, explore tide pools, visit the Pineapple Company for interactive exhibits, or enjoy family-friendly activities at resorts.

## Conclusion

As you bid farewell to Lanai, the turquoise embrace of its waters, the fiery dance of the setting sun on volcanic rock, and the warmth of the Aloha spirit linger in your memory. This island tapestry, woven with breathtaking landscapes, rich cultural heritage, and genuine hospitality, has undoubtedly touched your soul in a unique way.

Your Lanai story, crafted through adventures, encounters, and personal reflections, is now yours to cherish. Whether you explored hidden coves, reveled in vibrant hula dances, or simply soaked in the tranquility of secluded beaches, these experiences have shaped your understanding of this captivating island.

Let the lessons of Aloha- respect for nature, community, and cultural wisdom- continue to guide to guide you beyond your stay. Share your Lanai story with others, inspiring them to embark on their own island adventures.

# Travel Journal & Note

**Describe the sensation of walking barefoot on the warm Lanai sand, capturing the textures and temperatures.**

_____

_____

_____

_____

_____

_____

_____

_____

_____

_____

_____

_____

_____

_____

_____

_____

_____

_____

## How did the vibrant colors of Lanai's landscape- from turquoise waters to lush greenery- impact your mood and emotions?

_____
_____
_____
_____
_____
_____
_____
_____
_____
_____
_____
_____
_____
_____
_____
_____
_____
_____
_____
_____

# Describe the most memorable local dish you tasted, focusing on its unique flavors and ingredients.

_____
_____
_____
_____
_____
_____
_____
_____
_____
_____
_____
_____
_____
_____
_____
_____
_____
_____
_____

## Describe a moment of connection with the island's environment.

# NOTE

_____
_____
_____
_____
_____
_____
_____
_____
_____
_____
_____
_____
_____
_____
_____
_____
_____
_____
_____
_____
_____
_____

# NOTE

# NOTE

# NOTE

Made in the USA
Columbia, SC
04 September 2024

41332826R00065